OREGON

Sarah Tieck

Big Buddy BOOKS
Explore the United States

VISIT US AT
www.abdopublishing.com

Published by ABDO Publishing Company, PO Box 398166, Minneapolis, MN 55439.

Copyright © 2013 by Abdo Consulting Group, Inc. International copyrights reserved in all countries. No part of this book may be reproduced in any form without written permission from the publisher. Big Buddy Books™ is a trademark and logo of ABDO Publishing Company.

Printed in the United States of America, North Mankato, Minnesota.
052012
092012

 PRINTED ON RECYCLED PAPER

Coordinating Series Editor: Rochelle Baltzer
Contributing Editors: Megan M. Gunderson, BreAnn Rumsch, Marcia Zappa
Graphic Design: Adam Craven
Cover Photograph: *Shutterstock*: Anderl.
Interior Photographs/Illustrations: *Alamy*: Andre Jenny (p. 13); *AP Photo*: Phil McCarten/Picture Group via AP IMAGES (p. 25), North Wind Picture Archives via AP Images (p. 13), Greg Wahl-Stephens (p. 27); *Getty Images*: Jonathan Ferrey (p. 26), P. Gadomski/Photo Researchers (p. 30), Terry Smith/Time Life Pictures (p. 23); *Glow Images*: Wesley Hitt (p. 26), JTB Photo (p. 9); *iStockphoto*: ©iStockphoto.com/JerryPDX (p. 11), ©iStockphoto.com/outtakes (p. 30), ©iStockphoto.com/Willard (p. 17); *Shutterstock*: Lori Howard (p. 27), JPL Designs (p. 19), Jeffrey T. Kreulen (p. 27), Peter Kunasz (p. 5), Philip Lange (p. 30), LianeM (p. 30), Lukich (p. 11), St. Nick (p. 29), Josemaria Toscano (p. 9), Zigzag Mountain Art (p. 21).

All population figures taken from the 2010 US census.

Library of Congress Cataloging-in-Publication Data

Tieck, Sarah, 1976-
   Oregon / Sarah Tieck.
      p. cm. -- (Explore the United States)
   ISBN 978-1-61783-375-5
   1. Oregon--Juvenile literature. I. Title.
   F876.3.T54 2013
   979.5--dc23
                                    2012015707

OREGON

Contents

One Nation

The United States is a **diverse** country. It has farmland, cities, coasts, and mountains. Its people come from many different backgrounds. And, its history covers more than 200 years.

Today the country includes 50 states. Oregon is one of these states. Let's learn more about Oregon and its story!

Did You Know?

Oregon became a state on February 14, 1859. It was the thirty-third state to join the nation.

Oregon is on the Pacific Ocean.

5

OREGON UP CLOSE

The United States has four main **regions**. Oregon is in the West.

Oregon has four states on its borders. Washington is north. Idaho is east. Nevada and California are south. The Pacific Ocean is west.

Oregon has a total area of 97,048 square miles (251,353 sq km). About 3.8 million people live there.

REGIONS OF THE UNITED STATES

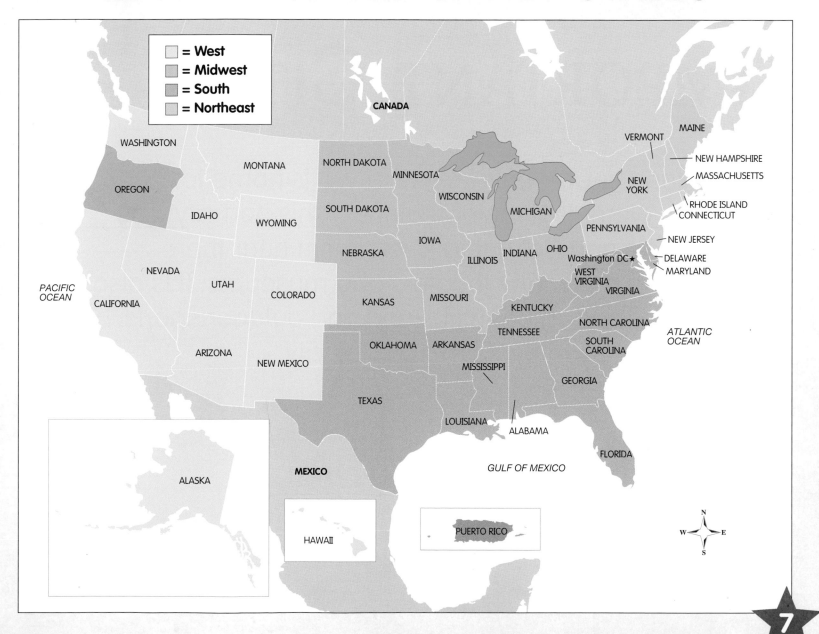

= West
= Midwest
= South
= Northeast

CANADA

WASHINGTON
MONTANA
NORTH DAKOTA
MINNESOTA
VERMONT
MAINE
NEW HAMPSHIRE
MASSACHUSETTS
OREGON
IDAHO
WYOMING
SOUTH DAKOTA
WISCONSIN
MICHIGAN
NEW YORK
RHODE ISLAND
CONNECTICUT
PENNSYLVANIA
NEVADA
UTAH
COLORADO
NEBRASKA
IOWA
ILLINOIS
INDIANA
OHIO
Washington DC★
NEW JERSEY
DELAWARE
MARYLAND
WEST VIRGINIA
VIRGINIA
PACIFIC OCEAN
CALIFORNIA
KANSAS
MISSOURI
KENTUCKY
NORTH CAROLINA
ATLANTIC OCEAN
ARIZONA
NEW MEXICO
OKLAHOMA
ARKANSAS
TENNESSEE
SOUTH CAROLINA
MISSISSIPPI
GEORGIA
TEXAS
LOUISIANA
ALABAMA
FLORIDA

ALASKA

MEXICO

HAWAII

PUERTO RICO

GULF OF MEXICO

N
W   E
S

7

IMPORTANT CITIES

Portland is Oregon's largest city. It is home to 583,776 people. Water is a major feature of this port city. The Willamette and Columbia Rivers meet near there.

Portland has many theaters and museums. It is also known for having beautiful land and outdoor sports. Mount Hood can be seen from the city.

Portland is called "the City of Roses." It has rose gardens, and a rose festival is held there each year.

Oregon

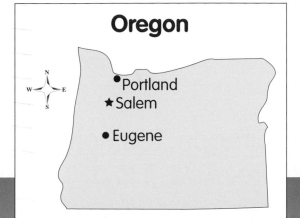

• Portland
★ Salem
• Eugene

Mount Hood is Oregon's tallest point. It is 11,239 feet (3,426 m) high.

Eugene is the second-largest city in Oregon. It is home to 156,185 people. Many artists live there. And, it is a popular place for biking and spending time outdoors.

Salem is the state **capital**. It is also the state's third-largest city, with 154,637 people. Salem is located in the Willamette Valley. This city is a leader in food manufacturing.

Eugene is near the Willamette National Forest.

The Oregon State Capitol was completed in 1938. Two earlier capitols were ruined by fires.

OREGON IN HISTORY

Oregon's history includes Native Americans, explorers, and settlers. Native Americans have lived in present-day Oregon for thousands of years. Spanish explorers first visited the coast around 1543. People then continued to explore the area. They discovered its rich **resources**, such as animal furs, forests, and water.

In the 1840s, many settlers came to the Willamette Valley on the Oregon Trail. Oregon became a territory in 1848 and a state in 1859.

John McLoughlin is known as "the Father of Oregon." He was a partner in a powerful fur-trading company in the area. He encouraged people to settle there.

Pioneers faced many dangers on the Oregon Trail. The land was wild and they had to carry all their supplies in covered wagons!

13

Timeline

1805

Meriwether Lewis and William Clark arrived in what is now Oregon. They explored the western United States after the **Louisiana Purchase**.

1848

Oregon became a territory.

1903

In Heppner, floods killed more than 200 people. This was one of the state's worst floods.

1800s

Oregon became the thirty-third state on February 14.

1859

1938

The Bonneville Dam opened. It produced power and allowed ships to travel on the Columbia River.

1948

Mill Ends Park was created in Portland. At 452 square inches (2,916 sq cm), it is the world's smallest park.

2012

The University of Oregon Ducks football team beat the University of Wisconsin Badgers in the 2012 Rose Bowl.

1900s

2000s

Oregon allowed women to vote. Abigail Jane Scott Duniway of Portland helped make this happen. The entire United States didn't allow women to vote until 1920.

Barbara Roberts became the first female governor of Oregon.

1991

1912

Across the Land

Oregon has mountains, waterfalls, lakes, cliffs, coasts, and forests. The state has 296 miles (476 km) of coastline. The Willamette Valley is west of the Cascade Mountains. Hells **Canyon** and the Snake River are on Oregon's eastern border.

Many types of animals make their homes in Oregon. These include beavers, pronghorns, salmon, and pheasants.

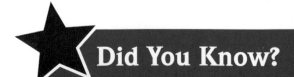

Did You Know?

In July, the average temperature in Oregon is 66°F (19°C). In January, it is 32°F (0°C).

The Columbia River forms much of the border between Oregon and Washington.

Earning a Living

Oregon has many important businesses. Some people work for companies that make computers and electronics. Others work for the government, do medical **research**, or help visitors to the state.

Oregon has many natural **resources**. The state's forests provide timber for building. Its rivers provide water and power. And, gravel and sand come from Oregon's mines.

Wheat (*above*) is Oregon's main crop. Other major crops include hay, potatoes, pears, and apples.

NATURAL WONDER

Crater Lake National Park is located in the Cascade Mountains in southern Oregon. It is home to Crater Lake. This is the deepest lake in the United States. It is 1,943 feet (592 m) deep!

People visit the forests and wild areas around the lake. These are good spots to hike, camp, fish, and cross-country ski.

Crater Lake is known for its clear water.

HOMETOWN HEROES

Many famous people are from Oregon. Author Beverly Cleary was born in McMinnville in 1916. She grew up in Yamhill and Portland.

Cleary wrote children's books. Her well-known books include *The Mouse and the Motorcycle*, *Ramona the Pest,* and *Runaway Ralph*. Some of her books are set in Portland.

★ ★ ★ ★ ★ ★ ★ ★ ★ ★ ★ ★ ★ ★ ★ ★ ★ ★ ★ ★

Cleary was a librarian before she became a writer. Her first book came out in 1950.

23

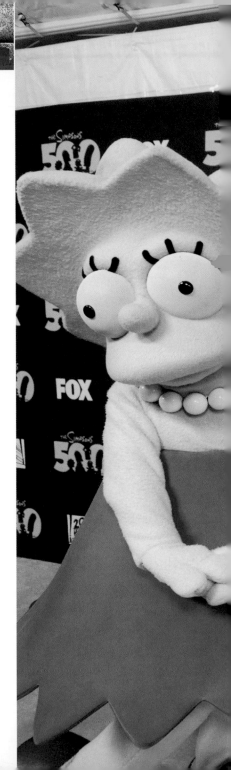

Cartoonist Matt Groening was born in Portland in 1954. He created a famous television cartoon called *The Simpsons*. This weekly series started in 1990. It is the longest-running cartoon show in history.

Groening (*center*) named the characters on *The Simpsons* after his family members.

25

Tour Book

Do you want to go to Oregon? If you visit the state, here are some places to go and things to do!

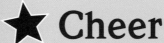 Cheer

Watch a college football game. Many locals attend University of Oregon Ducks versus Oregon State Beavers games. When these two rivals play each other, the game is called "the Civil War."

 Play

Try windsurfing on one of Oregon's rivers! This sport is especially popular on the Columbia River near the city of Hood River. This city is sometimes called "the Windsurfing Capital of the World."

 Remember

Visit the End of the Oregon Trail Interpretive Center in Oregon City. There, you can learn about pioneers in Oregon. They traveled in covered wagons and made homes in Willamette Valley.

 **See**

Visit Oregon's coast and see the Coast Range. This area features beaches, cliffs, mountains, and forests.

 Discover

Hike or white-water raft in Hells Canyon. This gorge is deeper than the Grand Canyon! Its deepest spot drops down 7,900 feet (2,400 m).

A GREAT STATE

   The story of Oregon is important to the United States. The people and places that make up this state offer something special to the country. Together with all the states, Oregon helps make the United States great.

The Cascade Mountains stretch from British Columbia in Canada to California. Some of the mountains are volcanoes!

Fast Facts

Date of Statehood:
February 14, 1859

Population (rank):
3,831,074
(27th most-populated state)

Total Area (rank):
97,048 square miles
(10th largest state)

Motto:
"She Flies with Her Own Wings"

Nickname:
Beaver State

State Capital:
Salem

Flag:

Flower: Oregon Grape

Postal Abbreviation:
OR

Tree: Douglas Fir

Bird: Western Meadowlark

Important Words

canyon a long, narrow valley between two cliffs.

capital a city where government leaders meet.

diverse made up of things that are different from each other.

Louisiana Purchase land the United States purchased from France in 1803. It extended from the Mississippi River to the Rocky Mountains and from Canada through the Gulf of Mexico.

region a large part of a country that is different from other parts.

research careful study of a subject in order to learn facts about it.

resource a supply of something useful or valued.

Web Sites

To learn more about Oregon, visit ABDO Publishing Company online. Web sites about Oregon are featured on our Book Links page. These links are routinely monitored and updated to provide the most current information available.

www.abdopublishing.com

Index